The Falling of Saturn

By: Shay Alexis

Would it be a crime

To say goodbye

One last time

With you holding me

And me feeling happy

For once in my life?

The faint scars on my wrist

Remind me of a time

When I had starry eyes

And bruised thighs

You make tears flow out of my eyes

Abusing me with looks & words

Hurting me with your actions

But for some reason

I still stay

Look me in my eyes

Tell me I'm fine

Hold my hand

But not too tight

And love me

Just right

Love is so complex

So, let's just stay friends

But please don't ever think

I ever stopped loving you

I ever stopped liking you

I ever stopped wanting to kiss you

I look outside

I see white

The coldness hugging me tight

Being my only friend

Dull eyes

Bruised thighs

I wonder why

I always cry

My thoughts are daggers

Hitting my skull

"Let me breathe"

I plead

They take hold

Pushing me down and around

Being in the clouds

With the vision of you on my mind

Tell me sweet things

Lie to my face

Hold my hand

And stay forever

Make it go away

Put your hands on my face

Pull me close

Kiss me

And be my escape

Memories flashing

Water splashing

Death rising

Society burning

With her sweet face

Pale complexion

Beautiful eyes

Brown hair

And her oval face

I wonder

How could one person be so beautiful?

- I'm in love with you (sorry).

Millions of thoughts

Running through my head

Wanting me dead

Will I give in?

His words washed over me like a hurricane

Making me feel something

Making me feel less alone

But the sad part is

He's in an eternal sleep

come back to us

Sing for us

Make us feel something

Make me feel alive

The vows

The cake

The gowns

The ring

The hair

The makeup

The guests all gathering

Your beautiful face

Saying “I do”

The clapping

The tears

Us going through the years

Me, being the dreamer I am

Can't comprehend how happy I'll be

To be yours forever

Lately I can’t sleep

Insomnia takes me

I think of being empty

Not feeling complete

My soul has been dark

You're the only reason that I’m happy

You make me feel like I can’t speak

You're the reason I’m asleep

You say that you love me

Is that true?

I'd give up everything for you

I'd live for you

I’d die for you

Don't take advantage

I want to make it last

You deserve more than the sky

Just close your eyes

I'll show you the future

With me not being in it

Can I kiss you under the night sky?

When the only light shining are the stars?

I'll show you my scars

Don’t cry

I love you

I'll hold you tight

I'm not going to die tonight

You take my breath away

Making me in a haze

“it's just a phase”

Lying to myself

Like always

I'm obsessin

I'm deppresive

I'm saddened

It happened

You're drifting

So I'll just see the memories

Flashing

Putting me in a haze

Telling me it's okay

That she did love me

The lies swallowing me whole

Until I'm nothing but

Memories

I look at you wishing you were mine

Mine to love

God

You’re beautiful

I'm surprised you haven't noticed

How much I'm in love with you

When we touch

I feel like I’m on fire

I feel the burning

When I hold you

I fall apart

Please be mine?

People will stay

People will love you

People will hold you

But beware

They can damage you

In any given second

I want to fall asleep

Under the blanket of stars

With you in my arms

And hold you

Until reality kicks in

My feelings are like a roller-coaster

It goes down

It goes up

It jerks me around

It makes me want to throw up

Most days

I can control the roller-coaster

But sometimes

It takes over

You are like the seasons

Beautiful but painful

I love you but I hate you

Cold then warm

Rainy then sunny

When your cold and rainy

I feel trapped

I feel worthless

When your warm and sunny

I feel on top of the world

You're complicated

But yet,

So beautiful

"I love you" I whispered

As the wind twirls

As the world spins

I wonder when

I'll see you again

Don't ever think

That I never cared

That I was never there

Don't put this all on me

You're still beautiful to me

Don't be sad

I'll watch over you

With tears in my eyes

And blood in my veins

I wonder when

I'll see you again

Picking up the pen has been hard

My feelings are more than words

They're like stars

A bunch of feelings scattered around

Surrounding one thing

Isn't it beautiful?

How one person can be your whole universe

It's kind of funny actually

All these feeling is surrounding one thing

I can't comprehend how I feel for her

I'm like a big constellation

Always circling her

You make me feel like shit

Feel like I'm not worth it

Like I'm nothing

But for some reason

I stay

The thoughts shedding

Running down my cheeks

Burning my eyes

And bruising them

The whimpers getting louder

I can't control it

I can't tame it

I hear you calling

"Please stay alive once more"

But you don't understand

Love has kept me alive

And

Love is going to be the reason I die

You’re the sun

You're the rain

You're the pain

I love you

But

You’re destroying me

Breaking me

Hurting me

My throat swells
My face turns red
I wonder what it would feel
If I were dead
What people would do
What people would say
If people would pray
I wish it could all
Just go away

I look at the sky

With tears in my eyes

Wondering why

I have to be stuck down here

On planet earth

I wonder how

It would feel if I could fly

With my hair blowing

And me yelling

I wonder

Why can't I be so free?

I look at you

You look at them

I talk to you

You'd rather talk to them

I love you

You'd rather them love you

Can't you see?

How

You're slowly kill me?

My tears are becoming a swimming pool and you're the one who's drowning. But what about me? I've cut myself open for many of you before. I know how this game goes. Ill overconsume you. Drown you with my insecurities. Why me? I always feel so special because they choose me. Is it out of pity? Is it because ill bleed myself dry for you? over and over again I'm the one in a grave. You cry on the casket and pretend like you cared. My rotting body just lying there. Maybe I've always been dead. The ghost of me lingers. I'll find another one of you. And the cycle will continue on forever.

Sometimes death seems better than the thoughts in my head. The pounding thought or the blank space in my head. Either way I'm not okay. I'll sit here and distance myself until they all leave. Because who could love someone like me? Some say death isn't the answer but what if it's been calling my name since age 10? What if, at the end of the day, it's my only friend? The comfort of knowing it'll be there holding my hand. Guiding me to the day I say goodbye. It's like it's clinging to me. Not wanting me to get help. Not wanting me to let go. Maybe I'll never let death go. Maybe I'll listen to it. The flirtatious whispers are so calming. Maybe I'll give in?

I've sat here and listened to all the self-help talks. I've done worksheets and talked it out. I've taken my meds and haven't done anything wrong. But still, I'm here not feeling "better." I'm starting to feel broken. Tampered with. Damaged. I want help. I want to get "better." Or maybe I don't? I don't know. Who am I? Shay? A ghost writer? A ratting person? Or am I even a person? People say to turn to God. But God won't help me. Who even is "god?" I'm definitely noy okay. But who really cares? Who will be there? Only me. Because it's always just been me. I'm not okay. How many times do I have to say it before you listen? How many times do I have to bleed? This is going to be a forever thing. It's time for me to accept it. Time for me to take the "help."

Your energy matched mine. The comfortability. The safeness. The trust. You made me feel like a forest fire. You made me crave you more & more. Your touch. Your lips. Your eyes. You. Maybe we'll never be together. Maybe I'm just obsessive. That's what they all have said. Funny though, you said it too. Why do I still crave you? Why do I crave you tongue in my mouth. Your hand on my thighs. Your deep eyes staring into mine. Fuck. Your voice. You saying you want "more" of me. God, I wanted more of you too. I wanted your whole body against mine. I wanted to feel your hands travel my whole body. I wanted to hear you moan for me. Knowing I was the only thing on your mind. I have to wake up without you. But you're the 1st thought at night and my 1st thought in the morning. I hope you feel it too. But I'm just passing by.

m not as skinny. Not as pretty. Greasy hair. Messed up teeth. Double chin. This is shay. And I don't even vant to be me. My personality is shit. I'm a piece of shit. The reason dad drank. The reason I made you nto a waterfall. I hate me. I avoid the mirror so I don't have to face the facts. I suck in my tummy and nagine being anyone else. That's all I want. To be someone else. To restart. Who is shay? Who am I? I uess I'll never know. I guess I'll just mop. My tears are a sea. All I want is to see me bleed. The red lines eminding me I'm alive. I don't even want to be alive.

I’ve turned into a monster. I don’t recognize me anymore. I'm an empty bottle that only gets full with others love. But they don’t love me. The concept “you can’t love someone until you love yourself” is such bullshit. I loved you until I stopped breathing. I loved you till I bled all over myself. I reached out fo you but you turned away. I saw the dark man hold your hand and tell you the truth. The real me. I yellec out that I love you. But yet you kept walking. Walking out of my life like everyone else. You said you were different. You said you could handle me. But the second you saw the real me, you ran. I'd run fron me too if I were you. I’m scared of me too.

My angel baby,

I never got to meet you. I never got to name you. I didn't even know you were inside me. If you were a boy or girl or whatever you wanted to be. I would've supported you with everything. Loved you with every breathe I take. My angel baby. My unborn angel. I would've tried to love you with everything I had. I would've cared about you the way I needed to be cared for. I would've loved you with every inch if my being. I would've been your mother. Your mom. Your life support. I wish I could've watched you grow inside me and outside me. I wish I could hold you. I wish I knew what you would've looked like. It's been 3 weeks for you to exit my body. All the blood I've bled lately is terrifying. But it's you. My angel baby. My 1st miscarriage. My 1st chance to be a mother. But I will always be your mom. Even now. It wasn't our time, baby. Mommy couldn't do it. But I promise mommy will always love you and think of you. I will love you till my last breath.

Signed,

Your mother

I'm never the one. But I'm not the one for you. I'm not worth it. I'm not the person you're going to feel safe with. I'm the one you put up with till you meet the one. I'm the one who will love you till you wish I didn't anymore. Until you get tired of me. Until you see the real me. Why am I like this? Why would I rather push you away? I don't think anyone should love me. I don't think anyone can love me properly. I'm too much. I was raised thinking things were my fault. So, when another connection fails, I automatically blame myself. I'm too much for you. You will see.

I wasn’t able to pick up the pen for a while. I wasn’t able to put my thoughts on paper. I couldn’t express me at all. Here I am now, 17 days into treatment. Am I feeling any better? Why won't anyone listen to my story? Why can't I talk about what happened? Why won't they listen? I'm like a bird in a cage. Just waiting to be released. Will I be able to fly? Or will the containment get to me? I wish I could say I know/have all the answers. But does anyone? I'm that still bird waiting for the day I can fully fly. Fully live. Treatment takes time, but time is my worst enemy.

hope and pray my recovery will be over soon. I miss the feeling of my bed. The feeling of waking up and nowing my best friend is in the other room. Knowing dinner will be made and Astro will try to eat it all. he feeling of home. The smell of wax melts and sometimes coffee. The smell of everything I've been raving. A home where there's laughter. I home where I know I'm safe. I took it all for granted once. Vouldn't let myself enjoy the fact I finally have a home. A home where I'm loved. I am loved. Which cares me. Being loved and cared for like I've always needed. Like secretly I've always wanted.

I wish I could scream at the top of my lungs. I wish I could be destructive. I wish you were mine. Is that selfish of me? To still want you? To still have you in my head? I can hear your voice in my head calling me a loser or nerd. Of course, not in a mean way. That's just how we were. I fucking miss you. I'm going to become a puddle of empty bones. I would be that for you. I'd do anything for you. I mean that. I hop you can feel me trying to connect with you. I genuinely believe you were my 1st love, the love that hurt the most. The love that could always pull me right in. I love you so much I think I'm starting to hate you

I don’t want to die. Isn't that crazy? I want to live. I want to feel the dirt on my feet. Feel the breeze of the wind flowing through my hair. I want to come home to my best friends and watch pawn wars. I want to wear a bathing suit to go swim in the creek and not give a fuck about what anyone else thinks. I want to do everything my depression and anxiety has limited for me. I want myself. And wanting myself is the best feeling. Feeling yourself slowly getting better feels crazy. I wish I could talk to 10-year-old shay and tell her everything will end up okay. Because it will end up okay someday.

I feel like the earth knows what I need. Can tell when I need its breeze to hug me. Knows when I need its gentle love around me. Nature is fucking amazing. Th energy is fucking intense. It's almost like it's transferring its energy through me. This is love. If I never find love at least I know the earth loves me. The trees. The luscious blooming flowers. It's always there. It's always catering to us. You just have to listen.

Your sweet words

Your soft lips

Your precious skin

You

Is this obsession?

Why can’t I get over you?

Why can’t I get you off my mind?

Why/how are you so perfect?

I would do anything for you

Just ask

I'll be the one for you as long as promise the same in return

You and I

Like it has always ben

You and I

Like what we’re used to

Give me another chance

I promise I'll give you the world

The thin white lines have always been my best friend

The gushing red has called for almost a decade

If I give in

What will happen?

What happened to us?

I loved you more than I could say

Maybe it was me?

No

It was you

And your perfect flaws

I hate you

I hate all of you

Fuck you

Death. My main motivation throughout my years. My main goal. To me, it seems like maybe it's always been there. Lingering. Haunting me. Letting itself be known. I can't count how many times I've tried to give in. From an early age I've heard it calling. Then you came along. For some reason the constant shriek of death was faint when you were around. You made me want to live. You made me want to beat it. Cliche, right? The thought that you need to have someone else in order to be happy. But that's the sad reality. I could go back to the beginning; I could talk about how amazing you were. How your presence made me feel at ease. How you knew how to make me feel like a fucking explosion. You were a big part of me. I sat up at night thinking of you. If you were okay. If you were happy. If you missed me. It was like my mind was on an endless loop of you. I don't remember the day I fell in love with you. Maybe it was the day we laid on your bed and you held my hand/grabbed my hand to reassure me. Maybe it was the day you looked at me in your living room and told me you loved my smile. Or maybe even the day you finally opened up to me. Honestly, who knows. I just know that you were my drug and I didn't ever want to lose what I felt when I was around you. Funny though, "was." Fucking past tense. Because who could ever truly love someone like me? Right? Who could love someone who put their all in for you? Who could love someone who constantly let you back in even though you didn't deserve me? Who could love Shay fucking Shawley? Not you. In the end, you showed me who you really were. I want to sit here and say that it all worked out. That even though I couldn't be with you I could still be in your life. I covered up my feelings. I covered up distinctly how much I liked you. I tried to change me for you. Maybe death would've been easier than the heartbreak that followed you. Maybe never meeting you would have been best for me. Let's see, if I never met you, I wouldn't have cried almost every night. If I would've never met you, I wouldn't have begged for the bare minimum. I wouldn't have gone through the hurt that you caused. Reflecting back, it wasn't me. I wasn't the problem. I tried my best for you; but it wasn't enough. I'm not the type to only talk about the bad. There were good moments too. Laughing with you. Joking with you. Hugging you. The butterflies I got around you. The making everyone think we were mad at each other but facetiming that night. God, I miss that. I miss the old you. Now all I have are the memories and the painful words you said before you left. Now I hear your side of things from other people. Now death is screaming at me once again but this time with more reasons. I try to hate you. The way you think you are so smug. The way you talk. The way you laugh. The way you hurt me constantly. But we both know me better than that. Maybe I will always love you. Maybe my heart will always ache when I see you. Maybe I will always have to pretend like everything that happened between us didn't happen. It's obvious you're over it. Over me. I know you did care once. I know you did love me once. Whether you like to admit it or not. But we both know it's over. I can't think of you anymore without being hurt. The lies. Betrayal. Games. Manipulation. Why me? I wasn't the only girl that wanted you. But you chose to break me. Do you understand how fucked up that is? Maybe it was because I was vulnerable. Maybe because I gave you the attention you wanted. I gave you my all and received nothing back but a one worded text at times. It doesn't matter anymore though. It's all over now. Death is back whispering in my ear and you're now whispering sweet nothings into hers. Meeting you made me think that death was the bad guy, but at least it's always there. Ready for me. Waiting for me. Yearning for me. Death is calling for me. And honestly, maybe it's time to pick up the phone.

It wasn't about the attention or even the knowing. It was the way he looked at me. The way he said my name. The way he would show me affection. It was his laugh. His eyes. His smile. God, that fucking smile. I never experienced something like that; wanting someone so much. It was demolishing.

I was screaming and begging you to listen

Just this once

Listen to my pleas

Listen to the way I'm drowning

Listen to my heart aching

All I've ever wanted was you

I remember the nights of nothing

The nights that we just looked at each other and laughed

It was pure bliss

It was bliss to be loved by you

The inside jokes

The way you could brighten any room

Your smile

The way you cared

You

You were my biggest heartbreak

The kind of heartbreak that you will always remember

That you will forever be impacted by.

I held onto you with every aching inch of me

I beat myself until I couldn't breathe

Loving you has been the most painful but yet angelic thing I've done

My body craves you

Your touch

Your scent

The way you look at me

You're all I've ever wanted in a person

I'd be lying if I said I wasn't in love with you.

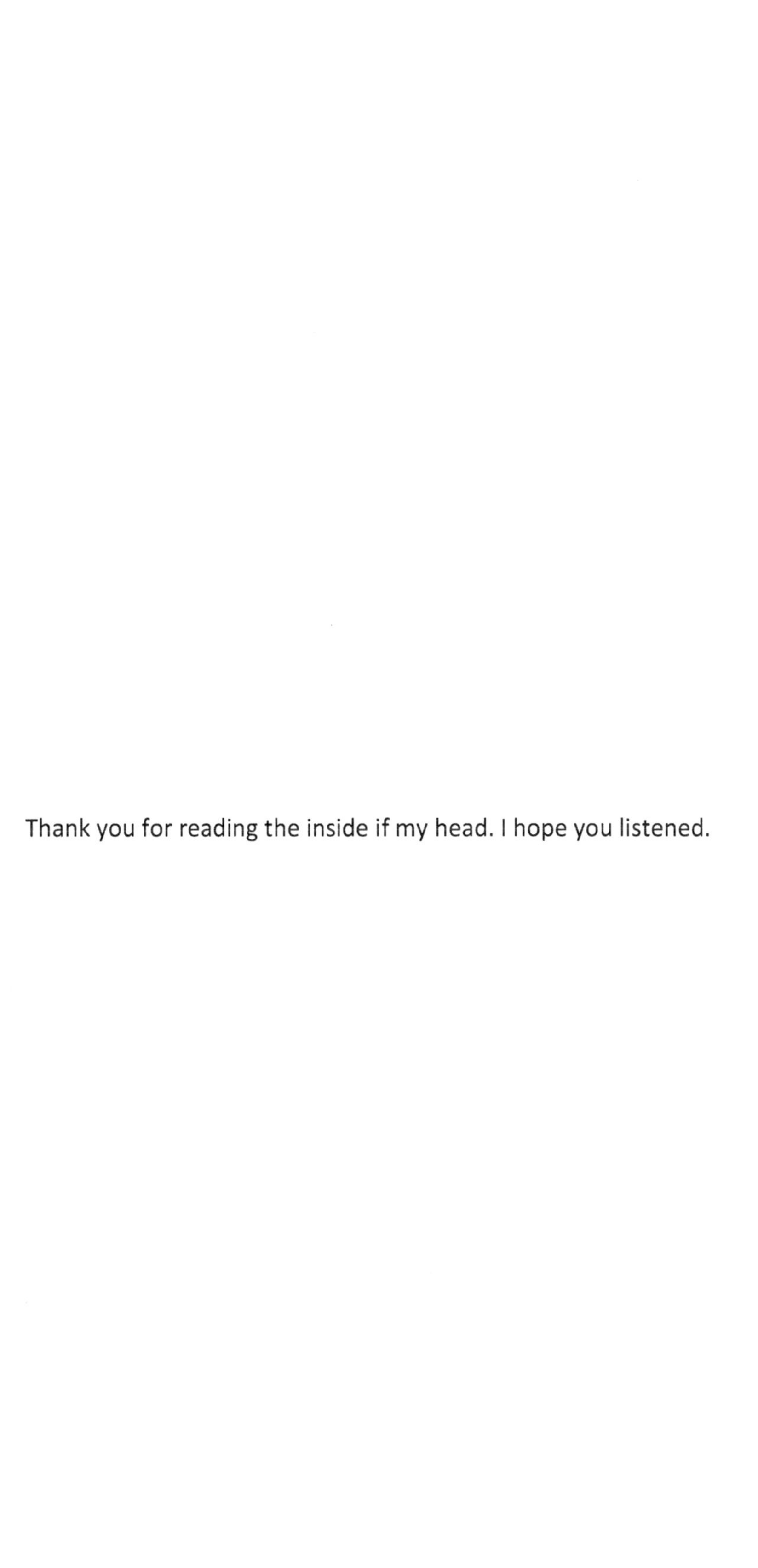

Thank you for reading the inside if my head. I hope you listened.

www.ingramcontent.com/pod-product-compliance
Lightning Source LLC
LaVergne TN
LVHW050345160826
845677LV00014B/3799

9798351120232